Services Framework
Design Guide

Services Framework – Design Guide

Designing the Solution

David Bright & Paul Freeman

Disclaimer

The content provided herein is for educational purposes and does not take the place of professional legal or business advice consultation. Every effort has been made to ensure that the content provided in this guide is accurate and helpful for our readers at publishing time. However, this is not an exhaustive treatment of the subjects. No liability is assumed for losses or damages due to the information provided. You are responsible for your own choices, actions, and results. You should consult your attorney for your specific publishing and disclaimer questions and needs.

Copyright

Table of Contents

Preface

Over the past few decades, we have developed a collection of guides to help IT solution provider companies provide repeatable, successful, and profitable customer engagements.

These guides are designed to assist IT solution provider companies in improving their service practice capabilities and to reinforce their current investments in people, process, and tools with best-in-class methodologies and approaches.

The guides provide solution provider employees, owners and managers with a "how to" approach together with essential information to determine what to implement, including executable action plans, tools, and templates.

Services Framework – Design Guide

This guide is focused on the design phase of the typical IT Services Lifecycle as depicted in the following diagram.

Services Lifecycle

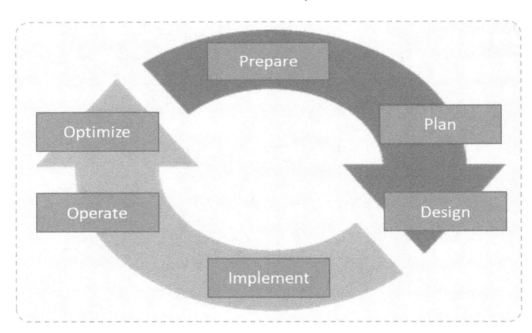

About This Guide

Guide Overview

This best practice document provides guidance to IT solution provider companies in creating a technical design framework for solution implementation.

The design framework specifies what the solution will include and how the various solution components will be connected into one operating whole.

Following the best practices described in this document will help your organization develop a structured, consistent approach to designing solutions.

Intended Audience

This guide is intended for new IT Solution Architects, new project and program managers, and for solution architects and project managers with expertise in other fields, who are transitioning into Solution Architect and PM roles in IT Solution Provider companies.

Why Is This Important?

With a well-defined, structured approach to solution design, your technical delivery team can consistently deliver solutions that incorporate technical and organizational best practices and build on the intellectual property and knowledge of your organization.

Having a structured framework for the design process will help your organization optimize the time to deliver and the customer experience. It will also enable you to address all aspects of the design process consistently across project, thus ensuring that all steps of the process are completed according to standards.

What are the measurable key performance indicators or skills required?

- Structured design framework defined and in place.

- Knowledge management system and processes in place.

- System design, physical design, device-level design, operations design procedures, and best practices in place.

- Planning processes in place for implementation, migration, staffing, operations, readiness, and support.

- Established acceptance criteria in place for the solution, training plan, and customer operations model.

- Solution designs produced consistently, according to best practices.

What is the list of measurable metrics?

- A services delivery plan and initial solution incorporating customer-specific infrastructure and vertical considerations has been developed. This includes:
    - o Physical design
    - o Feature/function design
    - o System design
    - o Device level design
    - o Operations design
    - o Implementation plan
    - o Operations plan
    - o Migration plan
    - o Staging plan
    - o Staff development plan
    - o Acceptance test plan
- Current state of the network assessed to identify the potential impact of the solution being implemented.
- Appropriate resources are identified and available.
- Staff fully trained and prepared to carry out the design plan.
- Customer and quality assurance have signed off on the solution design.

Overview

Designing a system or solution for a customer can be a complex exercise and will require a substantial amount of knowledge and expertise on the part of your technical delivery team.

A comprehensive system design provides an ever-present service that can scale to meet the customer's business growth and the adoption of new applications and technologies. Best practices system design typically considers technical and business requirements, including:

- Platform environment
- Compute environment
- Communications environment
- Cloud computing environment
- Network infrastructure
- Security
- Integration
- Customer growth plans and future needs

Deploying solutions entails a multi-phased approach that includes a discovery phase, an initial planning phase, a design phase, and an implementation phase. This approach is consistent with industry practices for business-critical projects. All requirements, designs, and network and operational remediation plans must precede the development of an accurate budget and implementation schedule.

A typical planning and design services offering consists of a suite of multiple service components. Its deliverables include everything needed for the successful implementation and subsequent hand-off of a fully operational solution.

Providing your customers with a planning and design service gives them a consistent and repeatable methodology to help successfully plan and design a best practices solution customized to their specific needs.

A staff development plan also should be included to help each member of the customer's organization prepare to use and support the solution. Figure 1 provides an overview of the design framework.

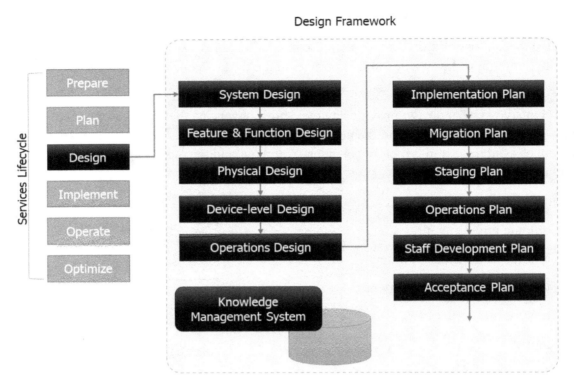

Figure 1. Design Framework

The design phase is a component of the overall Services Lifecycle. The design phase consists of several sub-elements that compose the design framework.

To provide a complete solution that describes all the necessary activities, meets the customer requirements, and has the prescribed features and functionality, you must create each component of the design framework for each engagement.

In addition to the design framework components, your organization should establish and maintain a repository of technical delivery content that is mapped to the suite of services your organization delivers to customers. You will use this content as you create each element of the design framework, and it will form the basis of the knowledge management system.

System Design as a Service

As a services provider, you want to sell solutions to your customers that encompass an end-to-end scenario. In addition, you may want to sell individual components of that end-to-end scenario to your customers as individual service offerings, or as part of a consultative service offering.

Since the design framework is a discrete service component that you can sell individually, you may want to consider offering it as a point service solution to your customers. During the sales cycle, this approach will enable you to stay connected to a customer if you become aware that the customer is considering the use of another service provider for the implementation phase. It also might be appropriate when you are building a new relationship with a customer who is not yet committed to the full implementation of a solution but is amenable to investing in the design phase.

Note that the same approach applies to the individual elements of each delivery framework within the Services Lifecycle model. In addition to offering a design service, you could offer the individual components of the design service. These component services might include systems design, physical design, feature and function design, device-level design, and operations design.

How is this valuable to customers?

If you can offer the design framework as a service, your customers will benefit from the ability to make a smaller initial investment without necessarily committing to the entire project. It also gives new customers an opportunity to evaluate the capabilities and competencies of your organization without having to commit to an entire project with your organization.

In some cases, the customer may decide to award the various aspects of a project to different service providers, thereby selecting the best vendor for each phase of the project.

How is this valuable to your Vendor Partners?

Your ability to offer individual design, implementation, support, and other services gives your Vendor Partners a way to better leverage your organization for specific customer opportunities that they might uncover. Your Vendor Partners also can offer joint service provider engagements for situations in which a customer has already selected an implementation vendor, but the vendor does not have all the necessary background and experience, such as design services.

What is the value to your sales team?

Your ability to offer both end-to-end solutions and individual services gives your sales team greater flexibility in positioning your service offerings to customers, depending on their specific needs, budgets, and implementation time frames. It may also provide a degree of differentiation between your organization and your competition.

If you are not able to offer individual services such as the design service, it may limit the number of engagements that your sales team can close. It also may provide an opportunity for your competition to win parts of an engagement if the customer is planning to separate out the various components of the solution to multiple vendors.

What is the relation to other services?

In the Services Lifecycle model, there is usually a logical flow between the various high-level activities comprising an end-to-end solution.

The discovery and readiness framework and all deliverables are inputs to the design framework. Therefore, each delivery framework must have very well-defined final deliverables. If you sell one stage as an individual service, it must consistently produce all the information required to support the following stage.

Because each framework should be able to stand alone, your sales team can sell individual framework elements; sell combinations of elements, such as the discovery and readiness framework with the design framework; or sell an entire end-to-end solution.

Prerequisites

Prior to initiating a design service, you should confirm that you have the required background information from the discovery and readiness framework phase available. If a vendor other than your organization completed the discovery and readiness phase, make sure that you have access to, and a way to validate, the following data and deliverables:

- Site Survey
- Site Readiness
- Network Readiness
- Platform Readiness
- Application Readiness
- Operations Readiness

Please refer to the Building a Discovery and Readiness Framework guide for more details.

Statement of Work (SOW)

While each service organization will have its own unique format and structure for the statement of work (SOW), you should include the following items in the standard SOW template for the design service:

- System design service and deliverables, including system design diagram.

- Feature and function service and deliverables, including a feature and function design document.

- Physical design service and deliverables, including a physical design diagram.

- Device-level design services and deliverables, including a device-level design document.

- Operations design service and deliverables, including an operations design document.

- Implementation planning service and deliverables, including a detailed implementation plan.

- Migration planning service and deliverables, including a detailed migration plan.

- Staging planning service and deliverables, including a detailed staging plan.

- Operations planning service and deliverables, including a detailed operations plan.

- Staff development planning service and deliverables, including a detailed staff development plan.

- Acceptance plan, including review and acceptance criteria.

Once these have been defined in the SOW and all prerequisites are in place, you can begin the design service phase of the customer engagement.

Chapter 1: System Design

System design focuses on how the various solution components are integrated and how the components should integrate with the customer's existing infrastructure, platforms and applications.

In general terms, systems design is the process and art of defining the hardware, cloud, virtual, and software architecture, components, modules, interfaces, networks, and data for a computer system to satisfy specified requirements. One could see it as the application of systems theory to computing.

A system consists of regularly interacting or interrelating groups of activities or elements that, when taken together, form a new whole. In most cases, this whole has properties beyond those found in the individual elements of the system.

Steps for Creating the System Design

In the context of designing IT solutions, you should consider the system design as the overarching technical design for the solution, with a focus on how the solution hardware and software elements relate to each other.

Creating the system design to provide a complete picture will help gain agreement from the customer staff assigned to the engagement and will help identify the specific areas that need to be addressed in more detail to turn the designs into reality.

The system design entails an iterative process of refining the various design elements and choices through a series of design workshops. The steps are as follows:

1. Review requirements from discovery and readiness assessments.

2. Collect all relevant information about the existing customer environment.

3. Create or obtain from the customer an existing system design in block diagram format, highlighting all key components.

4. Add the new components into the system design diagram in the physical and virtual locations that would be most suitable.

5. Conduct one or more workshop design sessions with the customer architect and other relevant customer staff to identify any potential issues with the new design.

6. Build into the design any changes that were identified, and create a new, more detailed system design diagram.

7. Discuss this updated system design document in a joint working session with the customer team.

8. Continue this iterative process until all parties agree that the system design is workable and most suitable for the customer, but always within the constraints of the original vision and scope for the solution.

9. Get sign-off on the final system design.

The iterative system design process can begin with a very simple, high-level diagram. However, in this high-level diagram, you should highlight the additional components with explanatory notes and keys so that the customer architect team can understand the high-level functionality of each major component and the interrelationships among them.

Through the iterative process, the system design should become more and more detailed until it represents or contains all information required for fully describing the overall system connectivity and functionality.

Note that apart from the simplest of situations, the system design will usually consist of not one single diagram, but multiple diagrams, where each provides specific details that relate to a certain aspect of the system design. All diagrams contain textual content that explain the overall purpose for the system design. When the system design includes a summary of the overall vision and scope, the reader has access to the full context and background.

In other words, the system design document can be considered a technical business plan.

While this best practice guide aims to describe the overall process and approach to the creation of the system design for an engagement, it does not include specific technical information about any of the individual vendor partner solutions (examples of vendor partners include Microsoft, Dell, Cisco, IBM, HP, Amazon, SAP, Google, etc.). The vendor partner websites for your strategic manufacturing partners contain a wealth of content on the specific technical details, including design samples and guidelines for each solution area. Please refer to the vendor partner websites for more information.

During the system design process, you should ensure that the customer architect and staff participate in every step of the design process.

The customer architect and team will have intimate knowledge of the existing environment and technology deployed, and a detailed understanding of the functionality of the required end solution. You must therefore obtain their signoff on the final system design.

Action Plan

Follow these action plan steps to implement this component of the guide in your organization:

Step	Action
Step 1.	Create system design checklists for each solution offered by your organization.
Step 2.	Create sample system design documents for each solution offered by your organization.
Step 3.	Create system design policies as appropriate for each solution.
Step 4.	Create system design template documents for each solution offered by your organization.
Step 5.	Publish all the above content to your organization's knowledge management (KM) system.
Step 6.	Verify that the checklists, templates, and policies are being used for all engagements.
Step 7.	Submit all new customer system design documents to the knowledge management system.
Step 8.	Be sure all system designs are signed-off by the customer prior to implementation.

Chapter 2. Feature Design

This aspect of the design process focuses on the features of the solution that you will be providing. In most cases, the customer will have a broader and longer-term technical architecture and strategy in place but will require only certain aspects of that strategy to be implemented now.

Your solution platform may be able to offer many more features and benefits than those the customer currently requires. In that case, you can position them as valuable additions to your offering, even if they will not be needed immediately.

You should therefore determine the specific features that will be incorporated into your solution to be delivered to the customer at this time.

Another aspect of feature design has to do with the scope of the current project. The customer may have certain constraints, such as time and resources, which currently prohibit the implementation of all desired features. In this case, as the solution architect, you should advise the customer on the most effective combination of features that will fit the customer's budget and resources.

Key Steps in Feature Design

The steps in this part of the process are as follows:

- Identify the key functional areas/departments within the customer's business that the new solution will impact.

- Identify the key components of the solution as defined in the system design.

- Determine all possible features of each component.

- List all the minimum features required from each component.

- If possible, extend the system design diagrams by adding the features.

- List all additional features of each component that could be incorporated into the design without modification to the existing system design or without violating the vision and scope.

- List all additional features of each component that could be incorporated into the design with minimal additional modification or cost.

- List all additional features of each component that could be incorporated into the design but that would add extensive modification to the design, or additional cost.

With this information in hand, schedule a working session to discuss these lists of features with the customer architect team. Be sure that the features are clearly understood, and then work toward identifying the final list of features to include in the final system design.

Also, consider that the solution may require the components to provide certain features. All components, such as operating systems, applications, cloud services, network, and hardware devices, typically come in a range of types, models or versions. Once you have determined the features for the overall system design, identify the most appropriate types, models or versions of the platform, software and hardware components based on the features they offer.

Be careful, however, not to "over-configure" the solution, as this may have implications on the overall licensing costs for the solution. Therefore, identify which features are necessary, which features would be good to have based on future requirements, and which features are not required and may add unnecessary costs to the solution.

This final list of features per design component then becomes the feature design for the solution.

As before, always ensure that the customer signs-off on this final feature design.

Action Plan

Follow these action plan steps to implement this component of the guide in your organization:

Step	Action
Step 1.	Create feature design checklists for each solution offered by your organization.
Step 2.	Create sample feature design documents for each solution offered by your organization.
Step 3.	Create feature design policies as appropriate for each solution.
Step 4.	Create feature design template documents for each solution offered by your organization.

Step	Action
Step 5.	Publish all the above content to the knowledge management system.
Step 6.	Confirm that the checklists, templates and policies are being used for all engagements.
Step 7.	Submit all new customer feature design documents to the knowledge management system.
Step 8.	Be sure all feature designs are signed-off by the customer prior to implementation.

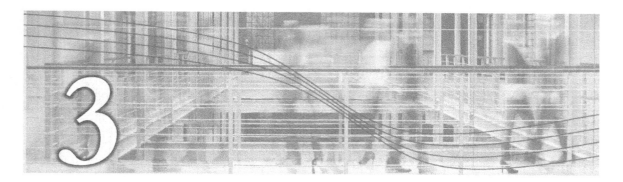

Chapter 3. Physical Design

This design element focuses on how the physical components of the solution interrelate and integrate together. The design guidelines should include the scalability and longevity of the solution, the customer's existing infrastructure and physical architecture, and the customer's long-term strategy.

When creating the physical design, begin with a review of the customer's existing environment. Include in the analysis the physical components that relate to your solution as well as all other components.

Also, note the physical premises, including the buildings, locations, physical access, and security systems.

Key Steps for Physical Design

The key steps associated with the physical design process include the following:

- Review site survey data collected in discovery and readiness phase.

- Collect information about the existing implementation, including hardware configurations, cabling, physical locations, addresses, etc.

- Create a diagram of the existing physical implementation.

- Incorporate the components of the new solution into the physical design diagram.

- Determine cable routing, hardware and software configurations, power requirements, routing, addressing, and other changes required to incorporate the new components.

- List all actions required.

- List all components required.

- Verify that all additional installation activities are included in the project plan, and that resources are available and allocated to complete the installation.

- Make provisions for any redundancy and fail-over scenarios.

As before, make sure that the customer technical staff participates in this design process and verifies the existing physical design. Ensure that the customer architect and technical staff approve the final physical design.

Action Plan

Follow these action plan steps to implement this component of the guide in your organization:

Step	Action
Step 1.	Create physical design checklists for each solution offered by your organization.
Step 2.	Create sample physical design documents for each solution offered by your organization.
Step 3.	Create physical design policies as appropriate for each solution.
Step 4.	Create physical design template documents for each solution offered by your organization.
Step 5.	Publish all the above content to the knowledge management system.
Step 6.	Verify that the checklists, templates and policies are being used for all engagements.
Step 7.	Submit all new customer physical design documents to the knowledge management system.
Step 8.	Be sure all physical designs are signed-off by the customer prior to implementation.

Chapter 4. Device-level Design

Once you have created the system design, it will be easier to understand which devices are included and what will be required of those individual devices. This is where device-level design enters.

Device-level design focuses on the various configurable elements of each device. As an example, when designing a solution that includes a compute server, it will be necessary to configure or "design" the server.

You will need to decide which type and how many network interface cards to install, how many disk drives to install, how to best configure the storage sub-system to meet the requirements specified for the server, and so forth. You then extend this approach to all devices in the solution, for example, the network hubs, network routers, and switches.

Note that while we are talking about actual physical devices in this example, the exact same approach is required for "virtual" devices as well. Even if a server is deployed as a virtual server on a cloud platform, the design process must still include all the configuration details for that virtual instance. Not only that, but the design will also need to include the management of those virtual devices and cloud-based platforms, which means designing cloud deployment and management solutions and processes.

During this phase, in addition to the device addressing and identification scheme, you should consider environmental and physical aspects related to the devices, such as cable specifications and routing, equipment racks, and power requirements.

You also will want to consider any systems management requirements during this phase. Note that in many cases, the device-level design phase will be included in the physical design phase, as these two aspects are very closely related.

Please refer to the technical documentation provided by your strategic manufacturer partners for the specific components that will be used in the solution. These documents provide all the details relating to the device-level configuration and device options for all individual devices.

Key Steps in Device Level Design

Key steps associated with this phase include:

- Identify and list all devices comprising the solution.

- Determine all device-level configuration settings and options for each device.

- Using the system design, and the features and function design, determine the appropriate device configuration and options for each device.

- Determine all addressing, software options, and configurations for each device.

- Create a device-level design document that lists all configuration and option settings.

As with previous steps, ensure that the customer technical staff sign-off on the final device-level design.

Action Plan

Follow these action plan steps to implement this component of the guide in your organization:

Step	Action
Step 1.	Create device-level design checklists for each solution offered by your organization.
Step 2.	Create sample device-level design documents for each solution offered by your organization.
Step 3.	Create device-level design policies as appropriate for each solution.
Step 4.	Create device-level design template documents for each solution offered by your organization.
Step 5.	Publish all the above content to the knowledge management system.
Step 6.	Verify that the checklists, templates and policies are being used for all engagements.
Step 7.	Submit all new customer device-level design documents to the knowledge management system.
Step 8.	Be sure all device-level designs are signed-off by the customer prior to implementation.

Chapter 5. Operations Design

Once you have fully implemented the proposed solution, you should verify that it operates correctly and continues to do so over time. The operations design phase addresses the overall operations of the solution.

Information technology (IT) service management delivers and supports IT services that are implemented in an organization. Service and solution providers not only verify that the solutions they deliver to customers meet the standard IT services criteria, they must continually improve their service management processes and best practices. Additionally, IT services should facilitate change as businesses evolve and compete in a global marketplace.

Businesses are increasingly dependent on IT service providers, such as your organization, to deliver standardized, predictable, quality services that support the business and enhance its responsiveness.

Providing those services requires service providers and IT organizations to have a clear understanding of where they are in relation to where they want to be, how they are going to get where they want to be, and how they will know when they have arrived.

Iteratively posing, answering, and acting on the answers to these questions constitute the fundamentals of continuous improvement, and the basis for operations design.

Key Aspects in Creating the Operations Design

When creating the operations design, consider the following aspects:

- Service Support
- Service Desk
    - Incident Management

- o Problem Management
- o Configuration Management
- o Change Management
- o Release Management
- Service Delivery
  - o Service Level Management
  - o Capacity Management
  - o Service Continuity Management
  - o Availability Management
  - o Financial Management
- Security Management
- Infrastructure Management
  - o Design and Planning
  - o Deployment Management
  - o Operations Management
  - o Technical Support
- The Business Perspective
- Application Management
- Software Asset Management

As you can imagine, the operation design requires strict adherence to policy and process since a simple error can have serious consequences.

It is also an area that is very well suited to standards and procedures. For more information, refer to online resources.

References

Operations design has been carefully studied and analyzed, resulting in a large body of information and guidance based on experience and application.

One of the best references to apply to the operations design phase is the body of knowledge available from the Information Technology Infrastructure Library (ITIL®).

This library is a framework of best practice approaches that facilitate the delivery of high-quality IT services. ITIL outlines an extensive set of management procedures that support businesses in achieving quality and value in IT operations. These procedures are supplier-independent and provide guidance across the breadth of IT infrastructure, development, and operations.

ITIL consists of a series of books, each of which covers a core area within IT Management. One of the primary benefits claimed by proponents of ITIL is the common IT vocabulary, consisting of a glossary of carefully defined and widely agreed-upon terms.

Information about the ITIL content can be found at https://en.wikipedia.org/wiki/ITIL.

Another important approach for services providers to research and apply to their organizations in IT service Management (ITSM).

ITSM refers to the entirety of activities – directed by policies, organized and structured in processes and supporting procedures – that are performed by an organization to design, plan, deliver, operate and control information technology (IT) services offered to customers.

Differing from more technology-oriented IT management approaches like network management and IT systems management, IT service management is characterized by adopting a process approach towards management, focusing on customer needs and IT services for customers rather than IT systems, and stressing continual improvement.

More information about ITSM: https://en.wikipedia.org/wiki/IT_service_management.

Action Plan

Follow these action plan steps to implement this component of the guide in your organization:

Step	Action
Step 1.	Research available methodologies and resources pertaining to IT operations.
Step 2.	Select a methodology or approach that best suits your organization.
Step 3.	Adapt and customize the methodology to suit your organization.
Step 4.	Publish your operations methodology to the knowledge management system.

Step	Action
Step 5.	Train all relevant staff on the methodology.
Step 6.	Create operations design checklists for each solution offered by your organization.
Step 7.	Create sample operations design documents for each solution offered by your organization.
Step 8.	Create operations design policies as appropriate for each solution.
Step 9.	Create operations design template documents for each solution offered by your organization.
Step 10.	Publish all the above content to the knowledge management system.
Step 11.	Verify that the checklists, templates and policies are being used for all engagements.
Step 12.	Submit all new customer operations design documents to the knowledge management system.
Step 13.	Be sure all operations designs are signed-off by the customer prior to implementation.

Chapter 6. Implementation Plan

The implementation plan focuses on the actual implementation of the solution. The solution architecture, solution design, device-level design, project management plan, security plan, and physical and premises data pertain to this phase.

The objective is the delivery of the working solution to the customer, as envisioned, within the scope of the project.

The implementation plan describes the sequence of specific steps and activities to be completed to achieve a working solution. It also includes resource and scheduling information to ensure that all tasks have the appropriate type and quantity of resources available to complete the implementation on time and within budget.

The implementation plan also includes sub-plans that address specific aspects of the solution, including the operations plan, the migration plan, the staging plan, the staff development plan, and the acceptance plan.

In most cases, the most practical way to create and maintain the implementation plan is to use a project management software application. In very large engagements, you may want to use a project portfolio management tool, or an enterprise project management application such as Smartsheet. These tools are better suited for managing all the sub-projects that comprise the full implementation because they:

- Perform scheduling and management reporting across all projects and sub-projects.

- Ascertain the status of all projects and sub-projects.

- Can quickly identify problematic situations and reveal the details of items that require attention.

- Can automate update requests to team members.

- Can automate project workflows and approvals.

- Can send automatic notifications to let the project manager and key stakeholders know when a task is at risk, or behind schedule.

Key Steps in Creating the Implementation Plan

In general, the key steps involved in creating the implementation are as follows:

- Gather all the final versions of the design documents that have been approved by the customer.

- Use the design documents to determine the major actions required for implementation.

- Use the design documents to determine the optimum sequence for implementation.

- Use the design documents to identify the resources required for each aspect of the solution.

- Identify the parameters of the solution scope, including the time frame and budget.

- Use a project management tool to create a high-level project plan.

- Confirm the high-level project plan with the project manager, design team, and customer.

- Once approved, expand the high-level plan into a detailed project implementation plan.

- Complete preliminary resource assignments with the resource manager in your organization and in the customer organization.

- Finalize the project implementation plan and get approval from the customer and the design team.

- Using standard project management methodologies, execute the project implementation plan.

- Use the project management tool to schedule and manage resource utilization to monitor progress.

As mentioned above, the overall implementation plan will typically include sub-plans covering migration, staging, operations, and staff development and testing. These are described in later chapters.

Action Plan

Follow these action plan steps to implement this component of the guide in your organization:

Step	Action
Step 1.	Create implementation plan checklists and templates for each solution offered by your organization.
Step 2.	Create sample implementation plan documents for each solution offered by your organization.
Step 3.	Create implementation plan policies as appropriate.
Step 4.	Create standardized implementation plan template documents for each solution offered by your organization.
Step 5.	Publish all the above content to the knowledge management system.
Step 6.	Verify that the checklists, templates and policies are being used for all engagements.
Step 7.	Submit all new customer implementation plan documents to the knowledge management system.
Step 8.	Be sure all implementation plans are signed-off by the customer prior to implementation.

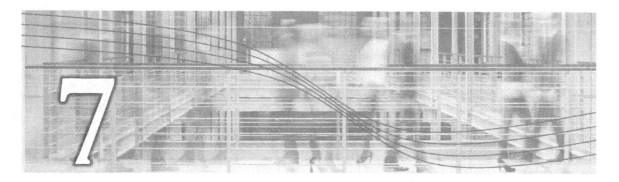

Chapter 7. Migration Plan

The migration plan is an optional part of the solution, needed only if the solution requires the migration of data or applications from the existing system to the new solution. The migration plan addresses all aspects of the migration to ensure that:

- All data is successfully migrated to the new solution.

- All required applications are operational on the new solution.

Key Steps in Migration Plan

- Analyze existing systems.

- Compile a portfolio of the existing applications, with version numbers and release levels.

- Identify all existing databases with the data structures, data schemas, and amount of data.

- Determine application usage.

- Determine data usage.

- Identify which applications can be eliminated.

- Test all other applications for compatibility.

- Determine which applications to remedy, which to replace, and which to migrate.

- Identify which data to migrate and which data to transform.

Once you have fully analyzed the existing applications and data and have determined which ones to migrate, you can formulate the migration plan.

To create the migration plan, start by completing the following activities:

- Determine how to migrate each application.

- Determine how to migrate the associated data.

- Determine how to test each application after migration.

- Create a test environment or identify a non-critical area of the customer's business to serve as a test environment.

- Conduct a test migration and analyze the results.

- Apply any remedial actions require to address any migration issues.

- Determine which and how many resources will be required.

Use this information to create the migration plan to be used during the implementation phase. This plan should include all the detailed steps required to complete the migration of the applications and the data.

Action Plan

Step	Action
Step 1.	Create migration plan checklists for each solution offered by your organization.
Step 2.	Create sample migration plan documents for each solution offered by your organization.
Step 3.	Create migration plan policies as appropriate.
Step 4.	Create migration plan template documents for each solution offered by your organization.
Step 5.	Publish all the above content to the knowledge management system.
Step 6.	Verify that the checklists, templates, and policies are being used for all engagements
Step 7.	Submit all new customer migration plan documents to the knowledge management system.
Step 8.	Be sure all migration plans are signed-off by the customer prior to implementation.

Chapter 8. Staging Plan

Although it may be possible to deploy a new system or solution in one complete operation, a complex system usually requires various parts of the solution to be implemented in stages. Once all stages have been implemented, the solution is complete.

The staging plan describes all stages in the full solution, details the steps required to complete each stage, and identifies items that have cross-stage dependencies.

Key Steps in Staging Plan

The key steps associated with defining the staging plan are:

- Use the design documents and the implementation plan to determine whether staging is required.

- Identify the high-level implementation stages, taking into consideration any dependencies that may exist.

- Identify the elements of each stage, including hardware, software, applications, networking, platforms, locations, and users.

- Determine the most optimal staging sequence.

- Identify the resources required for each stage.

- Build detailed instructions for the implementation and testing of each stage.

- Build staging details into the implementation project plan.

While it is useful to have a separate plan for the staging process, you should incorporate the actual activities into the master implementation project plan. That way, you can manage all aspects of the implementation.

Action Plan

Follow these action plan steps to implement this component of the guide in your organization:

Step	Action
Step 1.	Create staging plan checklists for each solution offered by your organization.
Step 2.	Create sample staging plan documents for each solution offered by your organization
Step 3.	Create staging plan policies as appropriate.
Step 4.	Create staging plan template documents for each solution offered by your organization.
Step 5.	Publish all the above content to the knowledge management system.
Step 6.	Verify that the checklists, templates and policies are being used for all engagements.
Step 7.	Submit all new customer staging plan documents to the knowledge management system.
Step 8.	Be sure all staging plans are signed-off by the customer prior to implementation.

Chapter 9. Operations Plan

The operations plan focuses on all activities required to verify that the implemented solution is operating according to the design.

You should base the operations plan on the operations design document and derive its detail from that document.

At a high level, the operations plan should include:

- Service support implementation details.

- Service desk implementation details.

- Service delivery implementation details.

- Security management implementation details.

- Infrastructure management implementation details.

- Application management implementation details.

- Software asset management implementation details.

Explain in detail all activities associated with each of these sections so that the delivery team will understand exactly how to implement them.

As with the staging plan, you should incorporate the operations plan activities into the overall master implementation project plan so that they can be managed with all other implementation activities.

Refer to the ITIL and ITSM material for additional background information on all aspects of the operations of complex IT systems.

Action Plan

Follow these action plan steps to implement this component of the guide in your organization:

Step	Action
Step 1.	Create operations plan checklists for each solution offered by your organization
Step 2.	Create sample operations plan documents for each solution offered by your organization.
Step 3.	Create operations plan policies as appropriate.
Step 4.	Create operations plan template documents for each solution offered by your organization.
Step 5.	Publish all of the above content to the knowledge management System.
Step 6.	Verify that the checklists, templates and policies are being used for all engagements.
Step 7.	Submit all new customer operations plan documents to the knowledge management system.
Step 8.	Be sure all operations plans are signed-off by the customer prior to implementation.

Chapter 10: Staff Development Plan

The customer staff that will be responsible for operating and maintaining a new technology solution typically requires additional training and readiness.

For this reason, the solution must include a staff development plan.

Steps for Creating the Staff Development Plan

Key steps associated with the creation of the staff development plan include:

- Use the design documents to identify which users and resources will require training and readiness.

- Be sure to include both end users and the customer support and IT staff.

- Be sure to include training and readiness on all aspects of the solution, including applications, devices, software, hardware, networking, platforms, configuration, use, and support.

- Identify the quantity and location of all the resources and users who require training.

- Using the master implementation project plan, identify when each training component will need to be delivered.

- Determine which training courses will need to be delivered where, when, and to whom.

- Determine if the training content already exists or will need to be created.

- If training content already exists, identify personnel or trainers who will be able to deliver the training.

- If training content does not exist, identify who will be able to create the content, determine the costs, and estimate the time required to create the content.

- Identify any training logistics such as venues, materials, and equipment that will be required to deliver the training.

- Create a training schedule that will ensure that the training is delivered to the right people at the right time and at the most convenient location.

- Incorporate the training schedule details into the master implementation project plan.

Note that while a substantial amount of training content is available from your equipment vendor partners and training partners, you may want to develop your own content that your organization can deliver.

This will provide another opportunity to differentiate your organization from your competition, as you will be offering a complete, end-to-end service to your customers.

However, bear in mind that it will require an investment on the part of your organization to create and update the content and have staff in-house capable of delivering the training.

Action Plan

Follow these action plan steps to implement this component of the guide in your organization:

Step	Action
Step 1.	Determine whether it makes sense for your organization to provide staff development services to your customers.
Step 2.	If your organization plans to deliver staff development services to customers, be sure that you have suitable resources in place and content available to deliver these services.
Step 3.	Contract with or form alliances with suitable training partners if required.
Step 4.	Verify that you have collateral, sales guides, and supporting content in place to help sell the staff development services as part of the normal sales cycle.
Step 5.	Create staff development plan checklists for each solution offered by your organization.
Step 6.	Create sample staff development plan documents for each solution offered by your organization.
Step 7.	Create staff development plan policies as appropriate.
Step 8.	Create staff development plan template documents for each solution offered by your organization.
Step 9.	Publish all the above content to the knowledge management system.

Step	Action
Step 10.	Verify that the checklists, templates, and policies are being used for all engagements.
Step 11.	Submit all new customer staff development plan documents to the knowledge management system.
Step 12.	Be sure that all staff development plans are signed-off by the customer prior to implementation.

Chapter 11: Acceptance Test Plan

In a technical solution implementation, the customer views the long-term vision for that solution in broader terms than any component or phase.

To be sure that customer understands and agrees to the full scope of a project:

- At the beginning of an engagement, communicate the scope of the project clearly.
- During the design phase, translate the original vision and scope correctly and appropriately into well-defined deliverables.
- Work with the customer to establish the need for a test environment or to identify the area of the business to be used for testing purposes.
- Summarize the final deliverables in the acceptance test plan. This is the list of deliverables that the customer will expect to see once the solution has been fully implemented.
- Identify the customer resources that will be responsible for validating the testing and verifying that the delivery acceptance criteria have been met.

The customer must approve the acceptance test plan prior to the start of the engagement.

Without the customer's approval on this plan, and without a strong change control process on the project, the entire project risks exceeding the schedule and budget.

Action Plan

Follow these action plan steps to implement this component of the guide in your organization:

Step	Action
Step 1.	Create acceptance test plan checklists for each solution offered by your organization.
Step 2.	Create sample acceptance test plan documents for each solution offered by your organization.

Step	Action
Step 3.	Create acceptance test plan policies as appropriate.
Step 4.	Create acceptance test plan template documents for each solution offered by your organization.
Step 5.	Publish all the above content to the knowledge management system.
Step 6.	Verify that the checklists, templates and policies are being used for all engagements.
Step 7.	Submit all new customer acceptance test plan documents to the knowledge management system.
Step 8.	Be sure that all acceptance test plans are signed-off by the customer prior to implementation.

Chapter 12: Customer Signoff and Quality Assurance

Once you have fully deployed the solution, completed all the training, put in place all of the operational aspects, and performed all of the acceptance tests, the customer can give final approval to the completed engagement.

Before the customer sign-off process begins, however, you must complete a quality assurance phase to validate that the solution has been implemented according to plan, and that all components of the solution meet the standards and quality expected for such an engagement.

Action Plan

Follow these action plan steps to implement this component of the guide in your organization:

Step	Action
Step 1.	Establish a formal quality assurance role within your organization and assign a suitable person to that role.
Step 2.	Implement a policy that requires every customer engagement to be reviewed by the quality assurance lead prior to final engagement closure.
Step 3.	Create customer signoff and quality assurance checklists for each solution offered by your organization.
Step 4.	Create sample customer signoff and quality assurance documents for each solution offered by your organization.
Step 5.	Create customer signoff and quality assurance policies as appropriate.
Step 6.	Create customer signoff and quality assurance template documents for each solution offered by your organization.
Step 7.	Publish all the above content to the knowledge management system.
Step 8.	Verify that the checklists, templates, and policies are being used for all engagements.

Step	Action
Step 9.	Submit all new customer signoff and quality assurance documents to the knowledge management system.
Step 10.	Implement a process to provide final engagement closure communications to the customer.
Step 11.	Implement a customer survey process to collect feedback from the customer on all engagements.
Step 12.	Be sure that all customer survey feedback is addressed. If the feedback is good, communicate that to the delivery team and the sales team. If the feedback is not good: ▪ Investigate to understand why. ▪ Follow up to remedy any problematic situations. ▪ Implement new policies to ensure that it does not happen again in future engagements.

Chapter 13: Automating Design Framework

Analysing completed engagements can help your organization discover ways of automating its design framework. Doing so will help you:

- Deliver consistent projects and solutions.

- Implement all solutions according to the same guidelines and best practices.

- Leverage organizational knowledge and intellectual property.

By codifying this standardized design framework and training all delivery staff on it, future engagements will produce predictable, efficient, and high-quality results.

Action Plan

Follow these action plan steps to implement this component of the guide in your organization:

Step	Action
Step 1.	Review all completed engagements to identify which aspects of the design framework are candidates for automation.
Step 2.	Create an automated procedure for each aspect identified.
Step 3.	Publish the automated design framework to the knowledge management system.
Step 4.	Make sure that the organization uses an automated design framework with a continuous improvement feedback loop.

Chapter 14: Vertical Designs

Horizontal solutions, such as data center designs and collaboration solutions, can be delivered in a standard fashion to most customers.

However, you may want to consider creating a suite of vertical solutions, which you can customize for specific industries, such as:

- Banking and financial services
- Retail
- Manufacturing
- Small and medium business (SMB)
- Healthcare, etc.

Creating vertical designs will provide your organization with a way to differentiate your offerings from those of your competition. At the same time, it will enable your technical and sales teams to build vertical knowledge and competency.

This knowledge can help your teams better understand industry-specific requirements and needs, and then build new vertical solutions to address those needs.

To create vertical solution offerings, you must address those scenarios from a technical perspective.

Action Plan

Follow these action plan steps to implement this component of the guide in your organization:

Step	Action
Step 1.	Review all completed engagements to identify which customer solutions can be reused for other engagements in the same vertical.
Step 2.	Review all engagements to identify opportunities to create vertical-specific solution offerings.
Step 3.	Create new vertical-specific design documents, templates, and procedures.
Step 4.	Publish all vertical design elements to the knowledge management system.
Step 5.	Make sure the organization uses vertical designs with a continuous improvement feedback loop.

Chapter 15: Design Deliverables

Determining exactly what to deliver to the customer for every phase of an engagement is entirely up to your organization to decide. It will generally depend on how structured your engagement processes are, what level of detail you are willing to commit to, and the overall quality of service provided.

However, you should consider the following deliverables to be standard for your design service:

System Design

- Existing system design diagram.
- New system design diagram.
- System design description document.

Feature and Function Design

- Feature and function design description document.
- Feature and function summary listing for each major component.

Physical Design

- Existing physical design diagram.
- New physical design diagram.
- Physical design description document.

Network Design

- Existing network design diagram.
- New network design diagram.

- On premise, Private Cloud designs
- Public and Hybrid Cloud Designs

Device-level Design

- Device-level design description document.
- Device-level summary listing for each major component.

Operations Design

- Operations design description document.

Implementation Plan

- Implementation plan description document.
- Master implementation project plan, including all sub-plans.
- Implementation plan description document.

Migration Plan

- Migration plan description document.

Staging Plan

- Staging plan description document.

Operations Plan

- Operations plan description document.

Staff Development Plan

- Staff development plan description document.

Acceptance Plan

- Acceptance plan description document.
- Acceptance plan checklist for each aspect of the system design.
- Sign-off summary sheet.

Final Hand-over Package

- Complete package of all final, completed deliverables in a hard copy and soft copy format.

Review and Approval

Each of the engagement deliverables should go through a review and approval process. The deliverables require review by the following parties, in the order shown:

1. Engagement manager or project manager.

2. Customer technical architect and customer sponsor.

The customer sponsor, or customer lead technical owner for the project, then gives the final approval for the deliverables.

Once all deliverables are signed-off, they should be made available to the team responsible for the implementation phase of the engagement.

Chapter 16: Knowledge Management

One of the most important elements of a successful services practice is the collection and management of unique, services-based intellectual property (IP) that an organization creates during the regular delivery of services and solutions to customers.

You should collect intellectual property in a repository of engagement processes and best practices using a process known as knowledge management (KM). Unfortunately, this element is often neglected.

Knowledge Management Benefits

There are several valuable benefits to collecting and managing this information, including:

- The ability to apply previously created knowledge to other engagements.

- The ability to create standardized, reusable components.

- The collection of engagement data for legal purposes.

- The formation of an internal knowledge network.

- The availability of real-life data that can be used for marketing and sales.

- The availability of real-life data that can be used for the creation of technical white papers.

- The availability of data that can support the "learning organization."

- A repository for the publication of standards and procedures.

- A repository of statements of work and other engagement management documentation.

- The availability of data to create a technical knowledge base and support management system.

- The availability of data to support a customer help desk.

Other benefits that may not be immediately apparent, but are equally important, include the ability to:

- Differentiate your services from those of your competition by responding more quickly to an opportunity or a technical problem.

- Retain knowledge within the organization following a period of attrition. When skilled, experienced employees leave the organization, their knowledge and skills also leave the organization. A workable knowledge management system helps prevent this problem.

Knowledge Management Systems

The knowledge management system can be very simple at first and may consist of a file sharing method or a portal site. It may develop into a more sophisticated, robust, and highly functional system, depending on the level of investment and the requirements of your organization.

Any and all engagement-related documentation should be stored and shared using the knowledge management system. These documents include reference architectures, sample designs, design guidelines, sample configurations, benchmark data, performance guidelines, security guidelines, status reports, and plans. When such content resides only on the engineers' laptop computers, your organization may be exposed to potential legal action if a customer issue arises.

One of the challenges associated with building an effective knowledge management system is determining a workable data taxonomy for the system. The content in the system must be categorized, tagged and labeled in a logical manner to make it easy to find information. This may require associating metadata, such as key words and categories, with each piece of content in the system.

While fully functional document management systems often have these features, you will need to invest time in determining the most appropriate taxonomy for your organization.

Note that the knowledge management system also can be used for training and readiness, such as to:

- Store online training courses, recorded training sessions, and self-paced training courses, which can be accessed through a training catalog hosted on the system.

- Keep track of training courses completed by staff and deliver and manage assessment tests.

- Store training certification information.

- Create and maintain certification exam road maps and development road maps for employees.

Deploying a fully featured, custom KM solution is ideal; however, you can build a workable system feasibly using an off-the-shelf software product such as Microsoft SharePoint Document Library. This version of SharePoint has all the key document management features, collaboration features, and knowledge network functionality required of a KM system. It is also extensible and can accommodate additional specialized requirements as your needs expand.

Action Plan

Follow these action plan steps to implement this component of the guide in your organization:

Step	Action
Step 1.	Identify the key functions and features of the knowledge management system.
Step 2.	Identify items to be included in the knowledge management system. These may include best practices, policies, designs, architectures, engagement documents, project plans, statements of work, training content, and so on.
Step 3.	Design a content taxonomy that is mapped to the content types
Step 4.	Deploy the infrastructure that will support the knowledge management.
Step 5.	Configure the system.
Step 6.	Upload the content.
Step 7.	Test the system.
Step 8.	Deploy the system to production.
Step 9.	Monitor the usage of the system.

Chapter 17: How to Measure Your Success

To gauge the success of your business, you should analyze and measure the effectiveness of the activities associated with each component.

Setting proper goals, evaluating staff performance, and measuring the positive or negative results of your business actions will help build success.

Likewise, measuring and evaluating the results after applying the concepts and practices suggested in this document will help determine the success of your business.

To measure the success of a solution design, you will want to measure the success of your implementation plan. If you have a proper design and implementation plan:

- The technical aspects of your solution work.

- You come in under budget and consistently have on-time delivery of the solution.

- The customer's goals and objectives are met.

- The customer has purchased the correct hardware, software and support.

- There are few or no out-of-scope items in your implementation.

In order to achieve this standard, at a minimum your company should:

- Develop a comprehensive design framework and toolkit that maximizes operational efficiencies and implementation consistency.

- Create, implement, and maintain standard policies through a knowledge management portal or an operations portal.

- Have a fully trained and prepared staff to carry out the design plan.

- Use many of the leading practices in this document to ensure proper design and execution of a solution.

- Leverage existing equipment vendor design templates and tools suited for the correct design and implementation of your solutions.

Implementing these design best practices, measuring the effectiveness, and adjusting your policies and procedures based on your evaluations, will help you improve the effectiveness of your design activities as well as the overall effectiveness of your solutions, thus producing positive results for your business.